Young Adult Literature

Magical Worlds

**Torrey Maloof
and Christina Hill**

Consultants

Timothy Rasinski, Ph.D.
Kent State University

Lori Oczkus, M.A.
Literacy Consultant

Publishing Credits

Rachelle Cracchiolo, M.S.Ed., *Publisher*
Conni Medina, M.A.Ed., *Managing Editor*
Dona Herweck Rice, *Series Developer*
Emily R. Smith, M.A.Ed., *Content Director*
Stephanie Bernard and Susan Daddis, *Editors*
Robin Erickson, *Multimedia Designer*

The TIME logo is a registered trademark of TIME Inc. Used under license.

Image Credits: p.5 Pictorial Press Ltd/Alamy; p.10 (left) INTERFOTO/
Alamy, (right) Robin Marchant/Getty Images; p.11 (top) Nomi
Ellenson/Getty Images, (bottom) WENN Ltd/Alamy; p.19 Flickr.com/
Public Domain; p.21 Moviestore collection Ltd/Alamy; pp.22–23 AF
archive/Alamy; pp.24,26 ZUMA Press, Inc./Alamy; p.27 Moviestore
collection Ltd/Alamy; All other images from iStock and/or
Shutterstock.

Teacher Created Materials

5301 Oceanus Drive
Huntington Beach, CA 92649-1030
http://www.tcmpub.com

ISBN 978-1-4938-3597-3

© 2017 Teacher Created Materials, Inc.
Made in China.
Nordica.052016.CA21600902

Table of Contents

A Powerful Spell

Why is the magical world so mighty and alluring? How does it cast such a powerful spell over readers? Magical **realms** are exciting and adventurous. They can also feel comforting and strangely familiar. Each story provides an escape from the stresses of everyday life. Reading fantasy novels allows readers to enter unique worlds. These worlds are full of curiosities and enchantments. And yet, even in these mystical realms, there is a sense of familiarity. At their hearts, despite the fantasy settings, these books tell deeply human stories.

Young adult readers connect well with magical worlds. On the surface, these worlds are nothing like their own. But readers see elements of themselves in the magical characters. This is even true when the characters are witches or wizards! Teenagers identify with the struggles and problems the **protagonists** face. They can relate to the challenging circumstances, even if the circumstances involve fighting a monster or flying on a broomstick. Young adults who are facing their own challenges can sink into the characters' worlds. The books may even help them feel as though they are facing their challenges with new friends.

Why is it so easy to connect to these new worlds and characters? Could it simply be . . . magic?

Before CGI technology created Gollum, he lived on the pages of J. R. R. Tolkien's books.

CGI Magic

CGI stands for computer-generated imagery. This technology brings many of the most-loved magical realms and characters in literature to life on the big screen. Of course, all the technology in the world can't hold a candle to your imagination!

There's No Place Like Home

Literary worlds can be magical. Sometimes, these fictional realms are packed full of **innovative** ideas and **mythical** beings. They are like nothing we have ever seen or imagined. Other times, they may resemble our own world at first glance. But the more you read, the more magical elements you find.

These magical realms are powerful blends of fantasy and reality. The young adults who read these stories often find ways to relate them to their own personal journeys. There are often **metaphorical** bridges in these stories that connect the two worlds. What a perfect setting for teens who are making the difficult transition from childhood to adulthood.

What Is Young Adult Literature?

Young adult literature is a genre aimed specifically at teenagers. While fantasy novels make up a good portion of young adult literature, there are many other subcategories to explore, including mystery, historical, dystopian, and contemporary.

Enchanted Escapes

Some magical realms are complete escapes from our world. J. R. R. Tolkien created a large fantasy world for his Lord of the Rings series. His stories take place on a large continent called Middle-earth. The land is full of mythical beings. There are elves, hobbits, and tree-like creatures called ents. The land is detailed and complete. Tolkien even made maps of his magical world!

Magical realms can be set anywhere, from faraway galaxies to **fathoms** below Earth in elaborate underwater kingdoms. No matter the setting, there is imagination, enchantment, and wonder. This is where the power of fantasy stories lies.

To Consider . . .

Authors who create complex magical realms have quite a lot to think about. Here are just a few of the many questions authors must consider when creating their magical worlds.

- ◎ What are the rules and laws of this society?
- ◎ What are the customs and cultures?
- ◎ What is the history of this world?
- ◎ What kinds of clothes do the characters wear?
- ◎ Are there schools for learning?

The Hidden Magical World

Magical realms are often connected to real-life locations in literary worlds. In stories, the magical world and real world often overlap in unexpected ways. The magic remains hidden and quiet. This entices readers to think that there may be magic surrounding them as well. They just can't see it.

J. K. Rowling's Harry Potter lives in a nonmagical village outside London, England. He is not aware that a magical realm even exists until he is accepted into Hogwarts School of Witchcraft and Wizardry. That is because it is hidden from nonmagical folks, or as Potter fans know them, Muggles.

Crossing the Threshold

Sometimes, protagonists can access magical realms from the ordinary world. Usually, they must cross through some sort of **threshold**. The threshold can be anything that allows entry into the magical realm. It can even be an ordinary object.

- Harry Potter travels to his magical school by a train that he boards from the secret platform 9¾.
- The Pevensie children enter Narnia through what appears to be an ordinary wardrobe.
- Alice first enters Wonderland by a dream and later through a mirror.
- Dorothy enters Oz by being swept up in a tornado.
- Bastian enters the land of Fantastica by reading a story and magically becoming part of the plot!

Isabella "Bella" Swan, from Stephenie Meyer's *Twilight*, lives in the town of Forks, Washington. In that town, teenage vampires and werewolves (or shape-shifters) appear to be normal people. They go to school, date, and fall in love. But the more you read, the more you learn about the hidden world of these mysterious creatures.

This is true in many fantasy stories. As you read, the differences between the ordinary world and the fantasy one become more apparent, even as they are made to feel real through the real-world connections. The more the reader learns, the more real the world becomes. In this way, young readers can connect to these new realms. The reader is lured in through the magical spells they weave.

Frenzy in Forks

After *Twilight* hit the shelves, tourists began **infiltrating** the tiny town of Forks, Washington. The previously quiet community is often swarming with fans who are eager to see the places described in Bella and Edward's world. The visitor center even distributes *Twilight* maps showing places of interest.

Creating a Magical Realm:
How Did They Do That?

Your Mission: Create an entire magical universe using only your imagination. Fun? Yes! Easy? Nope! Magical realms must be places where storylines can unfold naturally and where characters have room to live and grow. A magical realm is so much more than a location. It has to be unique, expansive, detailed, and well thought out. Here's how some of the pros have crafted their magical realms.

Ursula K. Le Guin

Le Guin's most powerful tool for creating fantastical worlds is her imagination. This can be seen in her Earthsea series. She states on her website that most of the research she does is into the "geography of (her) own imagination."

1940

1960

J. R. R. Tolkien

Tolkien stated that long before writing *The Hobbit* and The Lord of the Rings trilogy, he had "constructed this world mythology." He explained that he relied on maps to help construct his complex settings and stories. "If you're going to have a complicated story," he said, "you *must* work to a map; otherwise you can never make a map of it afterwards."

10

J. K. Rowling

The creator of Harry Potter confessed that she spent five years "constructing The Rules" for her magical world. She said, "I had to lay down all my parameters. The most important thing to decide when you're creating a fantasy world is what the characters *can't* do."

1990   **2000**

Christopher Paolini

To create the world of Alagaesia when he wrote *Eragon*, Paolini asked himself many questions. "Who might find a dragon egg out in the middle of nowhere? How did the dragon egg get there? Who else might be looking for the dragon egg?" Those questions and others helped him develop an amazing, mystical world.

11

Magical Sensibility

Magic, a common literary device in fantasy fiction, is often essential to the plots of the stories. What is it about magic that casts spells over young adult readers? What draws them deeper into the stories? Surprisingly, the answer lies in the *reality* of the magical realms. Reading about realms that feel real makes it easier for teens to connect to the stories and characters. It reminds them of their own lives and struggles.

Dragons ... Again?

Think about dragons. Since they are imaginary. You have obviously never actually seen a dragon. Yet you can picture one in your mind. Repetition of magical ideas and imagery, like dragons, can help them seem real.

Making the Unbelievable Believable

One key to writing fantasy is keeping it just real enough to be believable. These stories encourage readers to **embark** on magical journeys. The journeys serve as escapes from the familiarity of the readers' lives. For many young adults, routine days seem to blur into endless repetitions of school, homework, and extracurricular activities.

However, the power of fantasy realms is not just escapism. What makes these novels successful is their **realism**. For instance, Charlie, in Jenny Nimmo's *Midnight for Charlie Bone*, attends a special school. He must go to school, study, and take exams. Despite having magical powers, he and other magical protagonists still struggle with real issues. They may fight with their parents. Or they may have to find dates for school dances. Magic can help with a lot, but it will only get the character so far. Teenage problems remain problems whether the person is magical or not!

Magical Limits

There is a limit to everything, including magical powers. What would happen if magical characters had unending power? There would be no conflict and very little action as a result. Limited power helps create struggles in the stories. These struggles move the stories along. Conflict and struggle also help readers identify with the characters and make them relatable.

Some characters are born with magical gifts. In Rick Riordan's mythological series, Percy Jackson is the son of the mighty god Poseidon. But even he has limitations. He is impulsive and quick to anger. He needs time to develop and grow. But, his limitations help develop the story. He learns that his ADHD and dyslexia are signs of his godliness. As he learns, his magical feats start small. Then, they grow as his journey unfolds.

A Responsible Balance

In Le Guin's *A Wizard of Earthsea*, magic is everywhere. Those who are gifted in the magical arts can study wizardry at a special school. The more they learn, the more powerful they become. However, there are limits. The good wizards focus on remaining in harmony with the world around them. They must learn the consequences of their wizardry and strive to find the right balance between the darkness and the light.

Tools of the Trade

Magical realms often come with some pretty cool tools. From swords and spells to books and broomsticks, these tools can help or hinder the protagonists along their journeys. But the tools also come with rules and limitations. Some tools may only be used by worthy individuals. Others may only be used at certain times. Misusing magical tools may lead to dire consequences.

Amulets/Talismans

These items are small, often **ornate** objects with magical powers. They protect the people who wear them against attacks, but perhaps in limited ways. In the first book of the Bartimaeus trilogy by Jonathan Stroud, an amulet can only block magical assaults. It will not protect the person who wears it from a physical fight or minor injuries, such as a paper cut.

Broomsticks

Forget sweeping the floor, magical broomsticks are built for flying! Broomsticks are one of the better-known magical items. They appear in many magical stories. In *Hex Hall* by Rachel Hawkins, Sophie uses brooms to fly around with other witches.

Invisibility Cloaks

These special cloaks are magical pieces of clothing. When one is worn, it makes the person wearing it invisible to others. These cloaks allow people to hide from enemies, explore forbidden areas, or gain secret information by **eavesdropping**. King Arthur, Frodo, and Harry Potter all have cloaks of invisibility in their **arsenals**.

For Real?

Did you know the U.S. military and other scientific researchers are working on ways to make objects invisible? They are attempting to cover objects in special ceramic coatings. The objects would not physically disappear, but they would blend in with their surroundings. They would even be undetectable using radar.

Potions

There is a potion for almost every problem. Some potions heal sickness and wounds, like Lucy's cordial in C. S. Lewis's *The Lion, the Witch and the Wardrobe*. Others transform people's appearances. There are potions that provide magical powers. Other potions can conjure evil forces, and of course, there are love potions. Remember, though, many potions have side effects.

Rings

Magic rings can offer protection, immortality, or invisibility. But they can also be cursed and dangerous. Perhaps the most **infamous** magic ring is the One Ring from the Lord of the Rings trilogy. Sauron put so much of his dark power into the ring that he couldn't survive without it. The One Ring is able to control the other rings of power dispersed throughout Middle-Earth.

Swords

Magical swords are more than just weapons of steel. They sometimes help people perform tasks. They might even have special powers. In T. H. White's *The Sword in the Stone*, Arthur is the only one worthy of pulling the sword, Excalibur, from the stone. This magical sword later helps him perform great deeds throughout his reign.

Wands

Wands are usually depicted as long, thin tools. They are typically made from the wood of sacred trees. In T. H. White's The Once and Future King series, Merlyn carries a wand made from an exotic and sturdy wood. Other wands may be made of precious metals. C. S. Lewis's White Witch from Narnia uses a wand made of gold. Wands are used for a variety of things. They may cast spells, fight off enemies, or even partake in magical duels.

STOP! THINK...

Look closely at the first cover of *Peter Pan* (originally titled *Peter and Wendy*) by J. M. Barrie. Use the image to answer the questions.

- What details does this cover show?
- What magical elements does this cover include?
- What can you infer about this book from the cover?

The "Magic" of Friendship

Supporting characters are essential to good literature. These characters are often close friends of the protagonists. The friendships among the characters help make the stories realistic. This is another way fantasy tales cast their magical spells over readers. Friendships are key to making these tales relatable. After all, nobody relies on his or her friends more than teens do!

I'll Be There for You

Percy Jackson has many supportive friends that help him in his journey. One loyal friend is Grover Underwood. He remains by Percy's side, even when Percy makes questionable choices. An empathy link between the two allows them to communicate through unspoken emotions or even in dreams.

Some friendships form at the beginnings of stories. The bonds that tie the characters together never break. Readers may long for this kind of deep friendship. This model of devotion is something we all hope to find. It helps create a feeling of belonging.

Friends Until the End

In Tolkien's Lord of the Rings trilogy, Frodo decides to take a long journey. His best friend, Sam, pledges to help him and to remain by his side. Their **alliance** is tested along the way. But their friendship supports them throughout their journey and evolves as the plot moves forward.

Frodo and Sam

Finding Friends at Last

Some protagonists begin their journeys as outsiders or loners. They may be the new kids at school. Or they might be the only humans in a magical realm. Many young adult readers can identify with the anxiety of being new kids. They can also understand feeling alone. Teenagers may feel alone even when they're in the middle of a crowd.

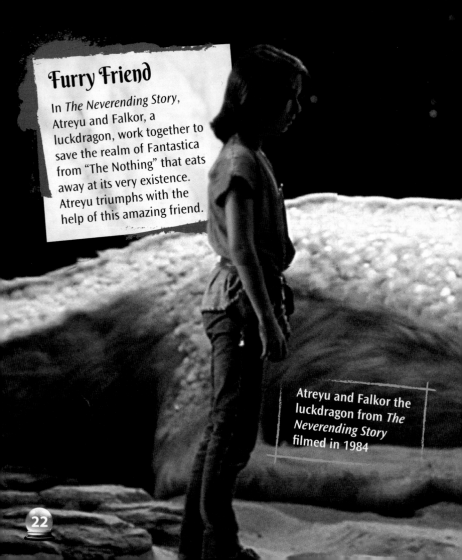

Furry Friend

In *The Neverending Story*, Atreyu and Falkor, a luckdragon, work together to save the realm of Fantastica from "The Nothing" that eats away at its very existence. Atreyu triumphs with the help of this amazing friend.

Atreyu and Falkor the luckdragon from *The Neverending Story* filmed in 1984

Lonely characters usually find friends along the way. These friends become the loyal companions who see the protagonists through their quests. In *Artemis Fowl* by Eoin Colfer, Artemis is a loner whose only real friend is his bodyguard. He fights an entire world of underground magical creatures. Later, one of the fairies, Holly Short, works with him to fight evil forces.

Steadfast Animal Companions

Sometimes, the most trustworthy friends are animals. This is especially true in magical realms. Magical creatures often serve as faithful sidekicks. They are always ready to lend helping hands (or paws, or wings). Animals can sometimes be more reliable than people. For some characters, it is easier to whisper fears and frustrations to furry friends.

The Wise Teacher

Most heroes in young adult fantasy literature are teenagers themselves. While teens may think they know everything, there is certainly more to learn. This is especially true in magical realms! Cue the wise teachers. These characters act as guides to help shape and **mentor** the younger characters on their quests for magical greatness.

Follow in my Footsteps

Many times, magical mentors are parental figures to the young protagonists. In *Eragon*. Brom trains Eragon in combat fighting, magic, and the art of the Dragon Riders. Brom's own experiences help him impart wisdom and knowledge to Eragon.

Eragon and Brom as depicted in the 2006 film

Protective Mentors

Magical mentors are typically older and wiser than the main characters. They can also serve as protective guides to help keep the protagonists safe. While these mentors are extremely powerful, they are usually only there to impart wisdom. The final battles against evil are up to the young protagonists.

But, not all mentors are much older than the main characters. In Kristin Cashore's novel, *Graceling*, Po is only a couple of years older than the protagonist. This does not stop him from being a helpful and wise mentor though. He encourages Katsa to find out the truth about who she is. He also helps her recognize how much power she has.

Glinda's Secret

In L. Frank Baum's *The Wonderful Wizard of Oz*, Glinda, the Good Witch of the North, is Dorothy's magical mentor. She gives Dorothy a gift—a pair of silver shoes. These shoes have the power to get Dorothy home to Kansas. However, Glinda does not tell Dorothy about the shoes' magical power until her journey in Oz is complete!

Choose the Right Path

Wise teachers do more than teach magic and provide protection. They also offer the protagonists codes of conduct to follow. These codes are based on **morality**. They are reminders that good triumphs over evil. If the heroes choose wisely, they will successfully conquer their obstacles.

Lion-hearted Peter

Aslan in *The Lion, the Witch and the Wardrobe* is a strong mentor for all the Pevensie children, but especially for Peter. As Peter begins his journey to becoming king, Aslan helps him discover his bravery.

In White's *The Sword in the Stone*, Merlyn uses magic to turn Arthur into different animals. Although humorous, these changes serve as lessons for Arthur. Each lesson lies in the experience itself! For example, when Arthur is a fish, he learns that he can use his wit to defeat a stronger enemy. In each situation, Arthur acquires wisdom. These experiences help shape Arthur's character as he grows up and remind him to choose the right path once he becomes king.

May the Force Be with You

The timeless fascination with George Lucas's Star Wars movies inspires many authors to pen stories in this galaxy. In Tom Taylor's *Luke Skywalker and the Treasure of the Dragonsnakes*, Luke's magical mentor is Yoda. According to Yoda, fear, anger, and hate all lead down the wrong path. He teaches Luke to focus his thoughts and energy on the good side of the Force.

The Magical Realm Checklist

The more fantasy literature you read, the more you notice certain elements that appear over and over again. How many books have you read that have wizards? Have you read more than one book that includes a magical sword? The next time you read a book about a magical realm, see which items on this list you can locate. You can even use this checklist to help you create your own magical realm.

Animals

- [ ] cat
- [ ] dog
- [ ] horse
- [ ] mouse
- [ ] owl
- [ ] snake
- [ ] spider

Magical Tools

- [ ] amulet
- [ ] book
- [ ] broomstick
- [ ] car
- [ ] carpet
- [ ] cloak
- [ ] elixir
- [ ] hat
- [ ] potion
- [ ] ring
- [ ] spell
- [ ] sword
- [ ] talisman
- [ ] wand

Creatures

- [ ] centaur
- [ ] dragon
- [ ] elf
- [ ] fairy
- [ ] giant
- [ ] goblin
- [ ] hobbit
- [ ] ogre
- [ ] Pegasus
- [ ] phoenix
- [ ] sea serpent
- [ ] troll
- [ ] unicorn

Supernatural Characters

- [ ] shape-shifter
- [ ] sorcerer
- [ ] vampire
- [ ] warlock
- [ ] werewolf
- [ ] witch
- [ ] wizard

Other

- [ ] seed
- [ ] tree

The Classic Conflict

The common literary **theme** of good versus evil is **prevalent** in many young adult fantasy tales. This timeless struggle helps draw readers into the story. That is because the conflict is relevant to all people, even in nonmagical worlds. Teenagers especially can face difficult choices every day. At times, making the right choice can feel like choosing between good and evil. It may seem like an easy decision to make, but that's not always the case. The dark side can be enticing! And, darkness can be deceiving. It may be difficult to tell who or what represents evil.

The Power of Darkness

Evil is always powerful. Dark lords are characters who have chosen to sacrifice good in favor of evil. Typically, these characters begin with good intentions and later experience some sort of a fall from grace. This leads them to the dark side. As they embrace the darkness, their identities change.

A New Name = A New Identity

When characters choose the dark side, they often form new identities. Sometimes, they are cursed with new names. Other times, changing their names is their choice. They hope that by choosing new, intimidating names, people will begin to fear them and their powers.

- In the Harry Potter series, Tom Riddle becomes obsessed with rejecting his Muggle family name. He changes his name to Lord Voldemort.

- In the Star Wars saga, Anakin Skywalker chooses the dark side and is reborn as the Sith Lord Darth Vader.

The Triumph of Goodness

Characters are often torn between choosing good or evil. This internal struggle is relatable to the real world. The moral of these fantasy stories is that **virtue** and goodness reign. In the end, the protagonist wins by choosing the right path and conquering the evil darkness or the villain.

Le Guin's Earthsea series is a great example of an internal struggle of good versus evil. Tenar is a priestess who lives underground. She is surrounded by darkness and the evil influence of the Nameless Ones. She is meant to assist in the execution of Ged, the hero. But when he arrives, she struggles to carry out the task. His kindness convinces her to spare him. Through much **turmoil** and internal struggle, she eventually sees the peace found in goodness. Ultimately, Tenar leaves the darkness behind and follows Ged into the outside world.

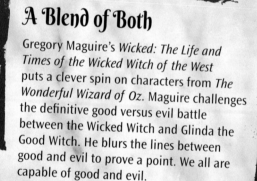

A Blend of Both

Gregory Maguire's *Wicked: The Life and Times of the Wicked Witch of the West* puts a clever spin on characters from *The Wonderful Wizard of Oz*. Maguire challenges the definitive good versus evil battle between the Wicked Witch and Glinda the Good Witch. He blurs the lines between good and evil to prove a point. We all are capable of good and evil.

The Journey

Most stories follow similar patterns. First, the setting and characters are described in detail. The plot moves forward, leading up to the major conflict. The **climax** of the story occurs when the action reaches a turning point. Then, the protagonist solves the problem. The story ends with a **resolution**.

All protagonists embark on some sort of journey as they move through this story pattern. The journeys may be literal voyages or internal journeys of self-discovery. Don't be fooled by the simple plot pattern! Fantasy stories often have many twists and turns. There may be countless conflicts along the way. Magical realms are **unpredictable**. That's one way to keep readers turning the pages!

The Saga Continues

Many fantasy novels are written as multiple books. There are six books in the Mortal Instruments series. There are four books in the Twilight series. It took eight books to finish Charlie Bone's story. And the stories of Oz include a whopping 40 books! But why is this? Fantasy realms are complicated. Because they differ from our world, it is important that they are described in great detail. Plus, these books appeal to huge numbers of readers who plead for more!

The Ultimate Boon

In his classic writings, including *The Power of Myth*, author Joseph Campbell describes the hero's journey well. He also shows how sometimes heroes are in search of items that will help resolve the conflicts that generated their journeys. They can only receive these boons, or vital items, once they have proven themselves worthy. This means they have to endure many **trials** and challenges before achieving success.

The Literal Quest

In some tales, the main characters' journeys begin in their homelands. Yet when the conflicts arise, the heroes must leave home in search of solutions. The journeys may be to obtain magical items. The characters might have to defeat evil wizards. Or they might need to rescue friends in trouble. Heroes might pass through magical forests, explore underwater kingdoms, or cross into new time dimensions. The beauty of the quest is learning more about the magical realms. And the excitement of the journeys lies in the adventures found along the way.

In Peter Beagle's *The Last Unicorn*, the Unicorn's journey follows this pattern. She leaves her forest on a quest to find other unicorns. She is afraid she may be the last of her kind. Along the way, she has magical encounters. She faces difficult obstacles. She also meets many unique characters. The heroine may be a magical unicorn, but her struggle to understand love and to find others like herself is a familiar **theme**. It is one to which many young adult readers can relate.

Who Am I?

At times, magical characters must go on journeys to discover who they really are. Laurel is the protagonist in Aprilynne Pike's *Wings*. One morning, she wakes up to find a huge flower blooming on her back. The journey she takes allows her to discover her true self among the faerie world hidden from humans' prying eyes.

A Journey through Space

In Madeline L'Engle's *A Wrinkle in Time*, Meg goes on a search through time and space to find her father. Along the way, she encounters many strange creatures and mysterious forces. This literal journey eventually takes Meg to other planets to fight against dark forces.

Most protagonists in young adult literature are teenagers. As their stories progress, they often age into early adulthood. This transitional time is tricky for the characters as well as for young readers. Emotions are heightened. Many experiences are first ones—first date, first love, first job. The protagonists are trying to figure out who they are. But through this time, teenagers gain independence and prepare to enter the real world. This theme of self-discovery also exists in the fantasy realm. Luckily, most fantasy characters have magic to aid them in their coming-of-age journeys.

In the Twilight series, Bella Swan is an average, awkward junior in high school. She is the "new girl" in school. In this way, many readers can relate to Bella. When Bella meets Edward (who happens to be a vampire!), she falls in love for the first time. Her journey is filled with drama, danger, and heartbreak. Yet, these experiences are what help her grow. They help her **mature** emotionally. Bella's quest is one of self-discovery.

What's Your Spirit Animal?

In Philip Pullman's *The Golden Compass*, each character has a daemon—an animal or creature that represents one's soul. Daemons are constantly shifting into different animals. This is because the characters are on journeys of self-discovery. Eventually, after the characters reach adulthood, daemons settle into specific animals that best represent the characters' personalities.

Magic Mountain Map

It doesn't matter who is in the story, where it takes place, or what it's about—stories in magical realms typically follow a similar pattern. The map is a framework to help you navigate the next magical story you read.

Going Up?

The action starts to build as the story unfolds. The protagonist faces conflicts and the excitement increases.

In the Beginning ...

Here's where we meet our protagonist. We get to know the who, what, and where of the story. The why and how of the magic is just starting to unfold.

The Summit!

This is the climax of the story—often the most exciting part! It is where the action shifts and the protagonist faces the core challenge head-on.

Going Down?

The protagonist solves the problem and resolves the conflict during this time. The hero is happy again!

In the End ...

At this point, the protagonist has learned something valuable and grown as a person. The story is nicely wrapped up, but the reader may wish for more as he or she faces the end of a great book.

What's the Magic Word?

There are so many enchanting and alluring elements at the center of magical realms. They all work together to create powerful, magical spells. These spells capture the readers' attention and take them along on journeys of discovery. At the end of those journeys, teenage readers are rewarded with deeper understandings of themselves and the world in which they live. They have been on long, sometimes grueling adventures with characters who might feel like good friends. Young adult readers may feel as though this journey has helped them through their own problems.

Readers come away from these stories with their own sets of "magical" tools that they can use. Those tools may be different for every reader. One may come away with more self-confidence. Another reader may harbor more courage. Still another may find validation. Each and every young adult's experience is different; however, most readers will agree that the journeys are definitely worth taking. So, when it comes to these books, what do you suppose is the magic word? Well, maybe it's two words: More, please!

Beyond Books

Books that take us to magical realms have become so popular that they have spawned blockbuster movie franchises. But that's not all. They've also inspired action figures, video games, landmarks, and even theme parks!

The Millennium Bridge in London is destroyed by Death Eaters in the film version of *Harry Potter and the Half-Blood Prince*.

THINK LINK

- How does a reader know that he or she is entering a magical realm?

- What purpose do magical tools serve in fantasy fiction?

- In what ways does life in a magical realm resemble life in the real world?

Glossary

alliance—a union formed to help both sides

arsenals—collections of weapons

climax—the most intense point in a story; before the resolution

eavesdropping—secretly listening in on other people's conversations

embark—to begin a journey

fathoms—units of length used to measure the depth of water

infamous—being well known for bad reasons

infiltrating—passing through

innovative—introducing new methods or ideas

mature—showing the emotional and mental qualities of an adult

mentor—a faithful and wise teacher or advisor

metaphorical—a figure of speech in which a word or a phrase is used in place of another to show similarity between them

morality—beliefs about what behavior is right or wrong

mythical—existing only in the imagination

ornate—decorative or fancy, usually with patterns and shapes

prevalent—accepted or common

protagonists—important main characters in stories who make good choices

realism—a style of art or literature that shows or describes people and things as they are in real life

realms—communities, territories, or kingdoms

resolution—the act of finding a solution to a conflict

theme—the core subject or message of a piece of writing

threshold—the point of entering or beginning

trials—tests of someone's ability to do or endure something

turmoil—a state of confusion, agitation, or commotion

unpredictable—incapable of being known before it happens

virtue—a good or moral quality

Index

Check It Out!

Listed below are the series and books from this reader as well as others you may be interested in checking out!

Baum, L. Frank—The Wizard of Oz series

Beagle, Peter S.—*The Last Unicorn*

Buckley, Michael—The Fairy Tale Detectives (The Sisters Grimm) series

Carroll, Lewis—Alice's Adventures in Wonderland series

Cashore, Krisitin—*Graceling*

Chainani, Soman—The School for Good and Evil series

Clare, Cassandra—Mortal Instruments series

Colfer, Chris—The Land of Stories series

Colfer, Eoin—Artemis Fowl series

Funke, Cornelia—The Inkheart trilogy

Le Guin, Ursula K.—Earthsea Cycle series

Levine, Gail Carson—*Ella Enchanted*

Lewis, C. S.—Chronicles of Narnia series

Maguire, Gregory—*Wicked: The Life and Times of the Wicked Witch of the West*

Meyer, Stephenie—Twilight series

Mull, Brandon—Fablehaven series

Nimmo, Jenny—Charlie Bone series

Paolini, Christopher—Inheritance Cycle series

Pike, Aprilynne—Wings series

Pullman, Philip——*The Golden Compass*

Riordan, Rick—Percy Jackson and the Olympians series

Rowling, J. K.— Harry Potter series

Steward, Trenton Lee—The Mysterioius Benedict Society series

Tolkien, J. R. R.—The Lord of the Rings series

White, T. H.—The Once and Future King series

Try It!

As an up-and-coming new author, you've been contracted by a publishing company to create an original story that's set in a magical realm. What kind of world will you invent? Refer to the checklist on pages 28–29 as you complete these steps.

◎ Draw a map of your magical world to share the setting. Make sure to include a key of important landforms, landmarks, and any other secrets your world might hold.

◎ How does the protagonist discover the magic in his or her world?

◎ What magical tools will be used?

◎ Who will be the antagonist? A person? An animal? A fictional beast? Draw a picture of this character.

◎ Describe the major conflict for the protagonist. What obstacles will be faced by the protagonist in the story?

◎ How will the book's conflicts be resolved?

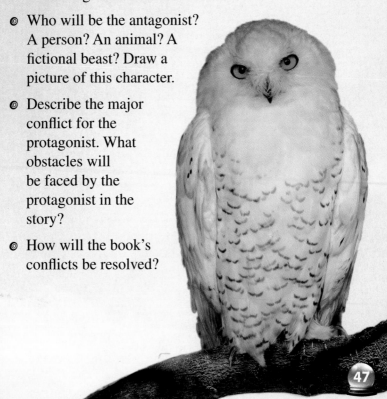

About the Authors

Torrey Maloof and Christina Hill have been BFFs for years and have much in common. They share a love of reading and consider Jane Austen to be their "wise teacher." They can often be found basking in the sun on a Southern California beach or with their noses buried in books at a local bookstore. Christina enjoys spending time with her husband and two young sons, who are all *Star Wars* fanatics. Torrey loves chasing after her young niece who loves all things Disney. The two friends love looking for the magical elements that exist in the real and hectic world in which they live.